Grammarly Help You Write Good Article

Bug Out Bag
Grammarly Help You Write Good Article

Mike Chiang

PUBLISHED BY:
Mike Chiang

Disclaimer

The information contained in this ebook is for general information purposes only. The information is provided by the authors and while we endeavor to keep the information up to date and correct, we make no representations or warranties of any kind, express or implied, about the completeness, accuracy, reliability, suitability or availability with respect to the ebook or the information, products, services, or related graphics contained in the ebook for any purpose. Any reliance you place on such information is therefore strictly at your own risk.

Chapter 03:Use Grammarly Tool

Chapter 01:Grammarly Introduction

The book we are going to introduce to you today is the "Grammarly" tool.
This is very good for people who do not have good grammar in English.

This is a handy tool for those who are not native speakers of English.
It is of great help in correcting the correct use of grammar.

(Image make by author.)

We can find it by typing "grammarly" into Google.
"Grammarly" is free to register and free to use.
"Grammarly" web site link is:
https://www.grammarly.com/
At the beginning of entering the site, if we are not yet a member, you can first register as a free member.
When we complete the registration, you will see such a picture.

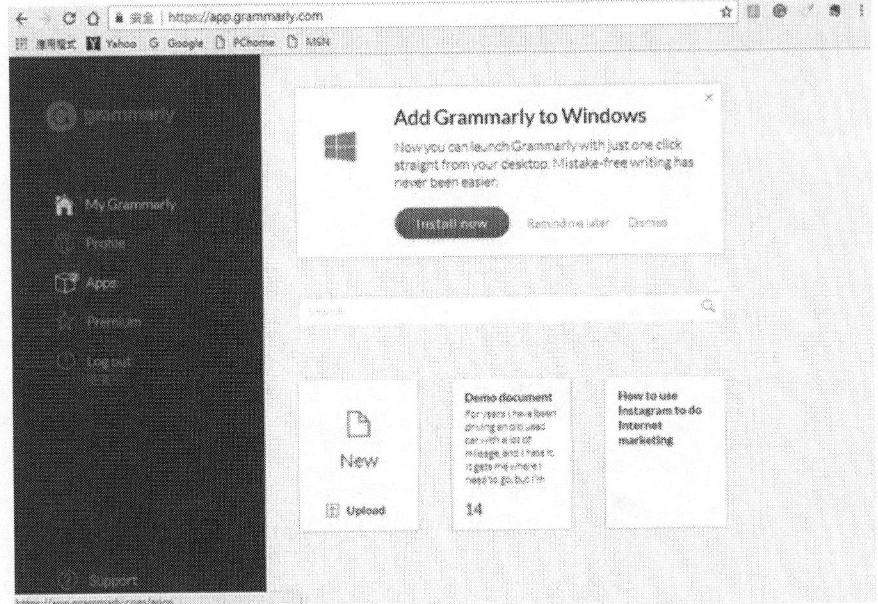

(Image make by author.)

The above is "Grammarly" in the web interface, the article will be introduced slowly behind the use of the method.

In the "Google Chrom" browser there are related extensions can be downloaded.

That's another version of Grammarly.

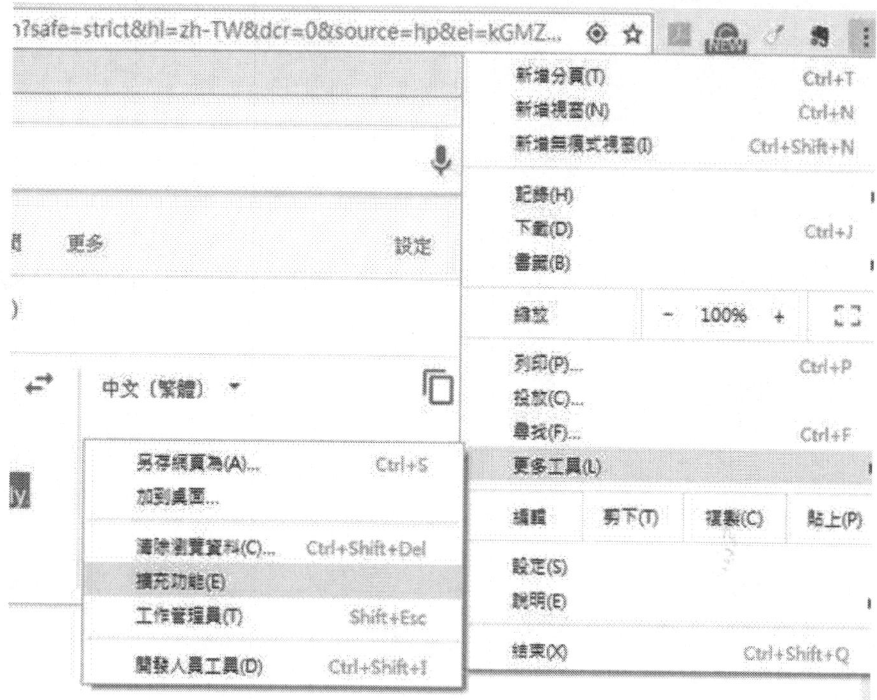

(Image make by author.)

In the "Google Chrom" browser, we can click the upper right corner of the screen.

More tools>>Extended functionality

(Image make by author.)

The browser opens a new page.

We first pull the new page to the bottom.

(Image make by author.)

Click "Get more features" link.

When clicked, it will open a new page again.

(Image make by author.)

The page we see looks like this.

This is the Google Chrom online application store.

We enter the keyword "grammarly" in the store.

(Image make by author.)

We can extend the program to Google Chrom's browser.

After the successful expansion of the picture.

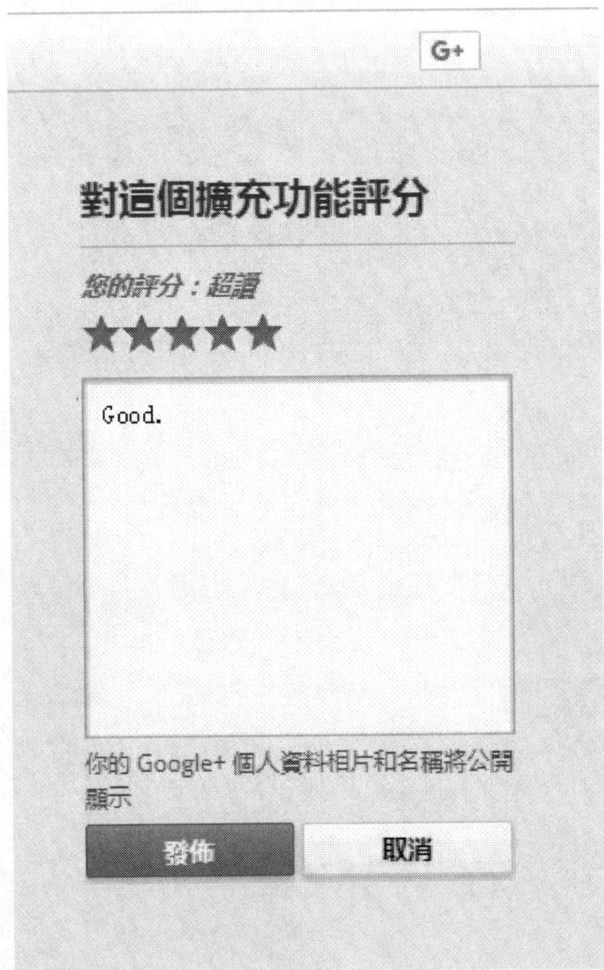

(Image make by author.)

We can also send our own ratings and opinions on this app.

Chapter 02:Google Search

We can also rely on search engine reference grammar accuracy.
This is another easy way.

(Image make by author.)
We first came to the "Google" translation screen, enter the sentence you want to translate.
After that, enter the search engine for the sentence you want to validate.

(Image make by author.)
The number of search results "459000000".

When we look at the results of a large number of words, the accuracy of the sentence on behalf of the high, the error rate is small.
We will search for another method.
This reference with the "SEO" method, preceded by "intitle:" keyword search.

(Image make by author.)
The number of search results "6440000".
This time the search range less than the previous, but also improve the accuracy of the search.

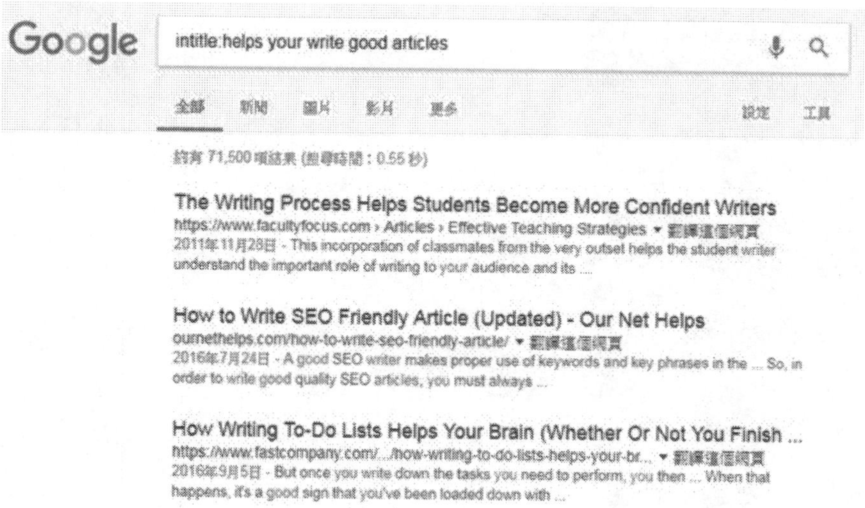

Google intitle:helps your write good articles

全部 新聞 圖片 影片 更多 設定 工具

約有 71,500 項結果 (搜尋時間：0.55 秒)

The Writing Process Helps Students Become More Confident Writers
https://www.facultyfocus.com › Articles › Effective Teaching Strategies ▾ 翻譯這個網頁
2011年11月28日 - This incorporation of classmates from the very outset helps the student writer understand the important role of writing to your audience and its ...

How to Write SEO Friendly Article (Updated) - Our Net Helps
ournethelps.com/how-to-write-seo-friendly-article/ ▾ 翻譯這個網頁
2016年7月24日 - A good SEO writer makes proper use of keywords and key phrases in the ... So, in order to write good quality SEO articles, you must always ...

How Writing To-Do Lists Helps Your Brain (Whether Or Not You Finish ...
https://www.fastcompany.com/.../how-writing-to-do-lists-helps-your-br... ▾ 翻譯這個網頁
2016年9月5日 - But once you write down the tasks you need to perform, you then ... When that happens, it's a good sign that you've been loaded down with ...

(Image make by author.)

We search for keywords again.

This time we deliberately wrote the wrong sentence.
See how the result is.
The number of search results "71500".
This time the number is indeed very small.
Probably mean: when we adjust the grammar of the sentence to do the search, when the number of sentences is significantly less, the grammar that represents us is wrong.

Chapter 03:Use Grammarly Tool

This time, we use the "Grammarly" tool.

We use "Grammarly" web interface as a demonstration.
Link to:
https://app.grammarly.com

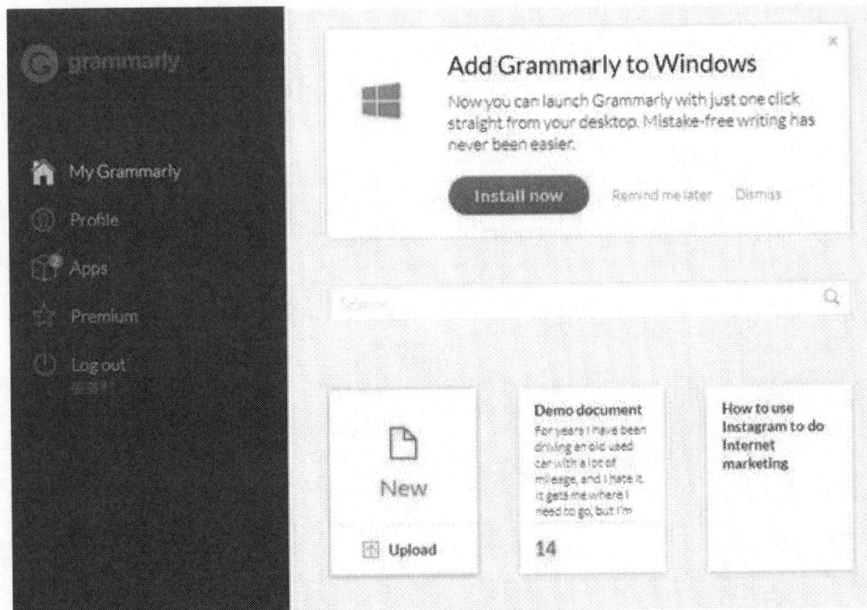

(Image make by author.)

Click "New" to open a new project.

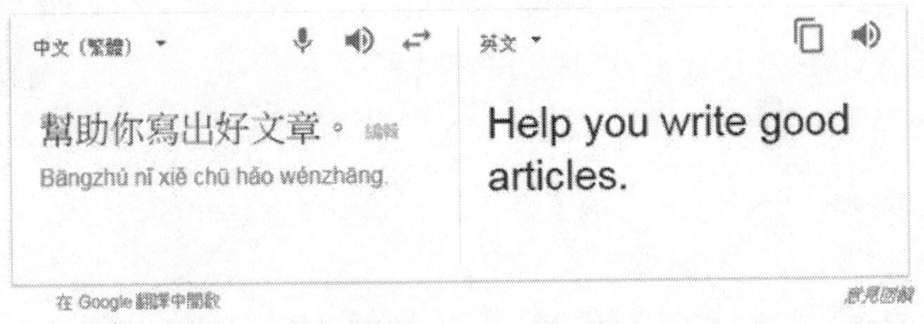

(Image make by author.)

We translate the sentence.

Copy the sentence.

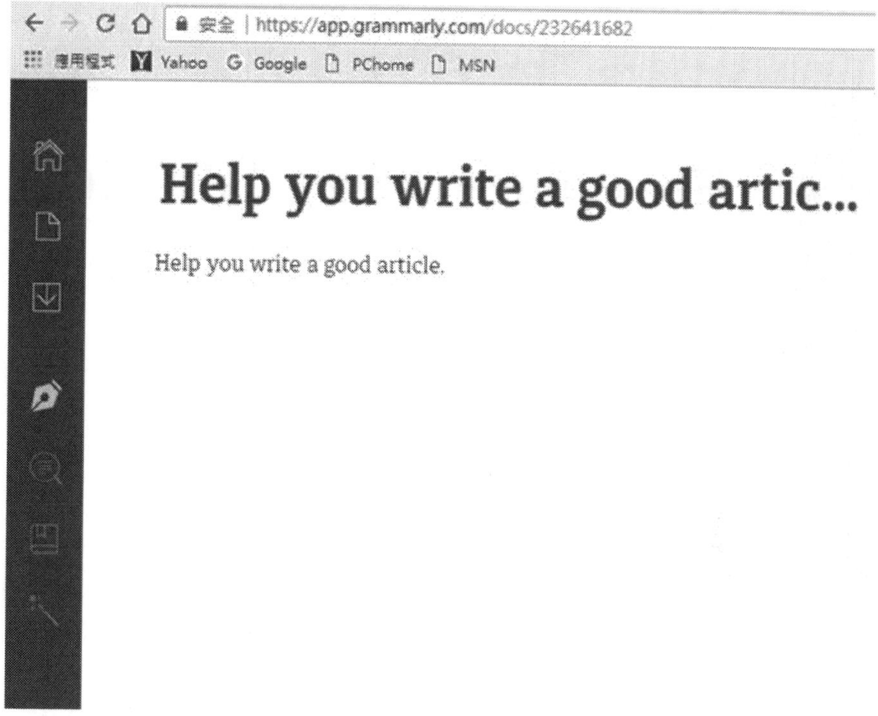

(Image make by author.)

The grammar that represents the sentence is correct when no prompt appears.

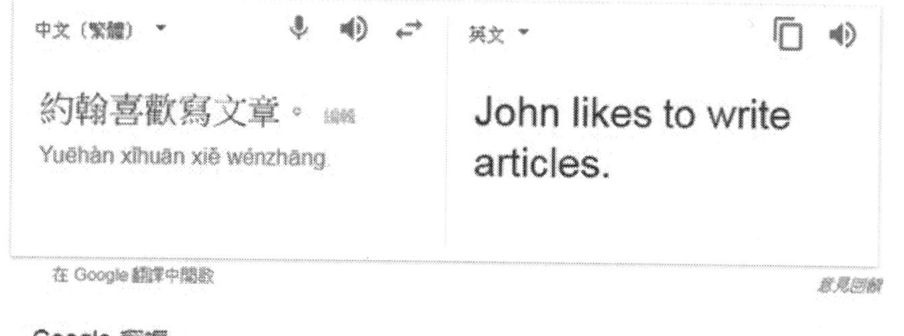

(Image make by author.)

Copy the sentence.

Paste the sentence.

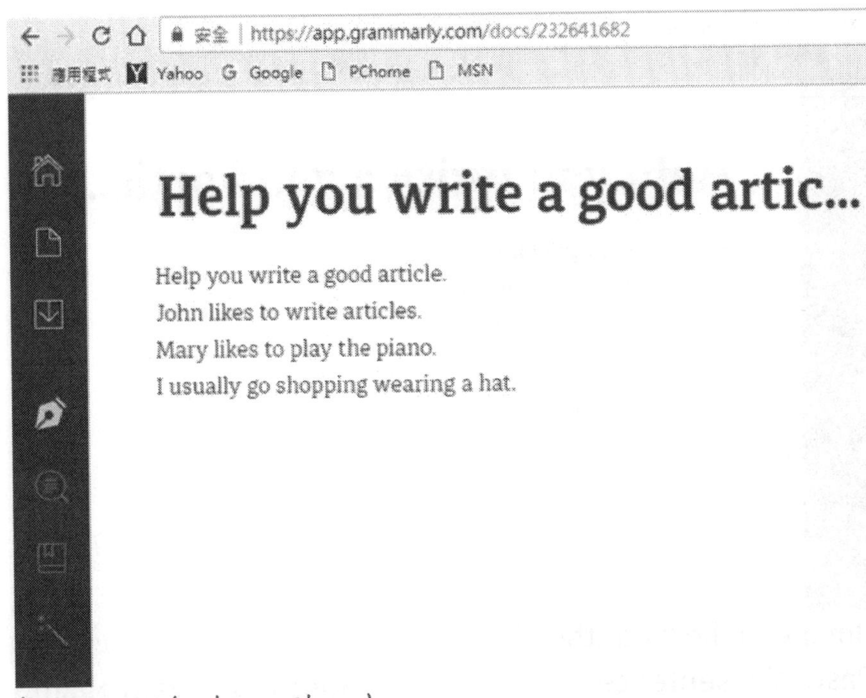

(Image make by author.)

Paste the sentence.

The grammar that represents the sentence is correct when no prompt appears.

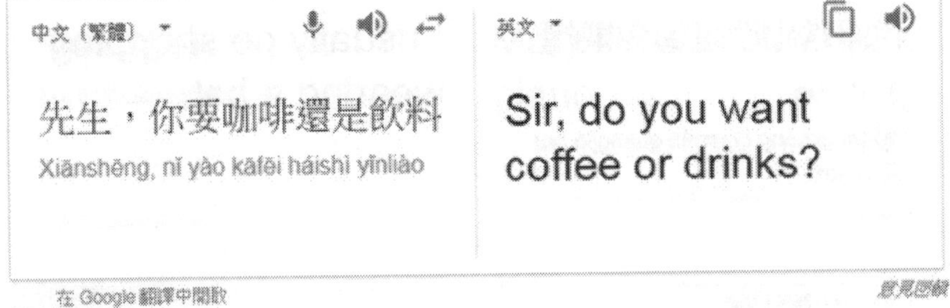

(Image make by author.)

Copy the sentence.

(Image make by author.)

Paste the sentence.

The grammar that represents the sentence is correct when no prompt appears.

(Image make by author.)

Copy the sentence.

(Image make by author.)

Paste the sentence.

The grammar that represents the sentence is correct when no prompt appears.

We deliberately added "the a" to the list of "boots."

When I go out in winter, I wear the a boots. the a → the

(Image make by author.)

When the sentence grammar goes wrong, it prompts to give you the correct reference.

Sir, do you want coffee or drinks?

When I go out in winter, I wear the a boots.

(Image make by author.)

And we just click it, it will help you fix it.

Sir, do you want coffee or drinks?

When I go out in winter, I wear the boots.

(Image make by author.)

Change back to the correct sentence.

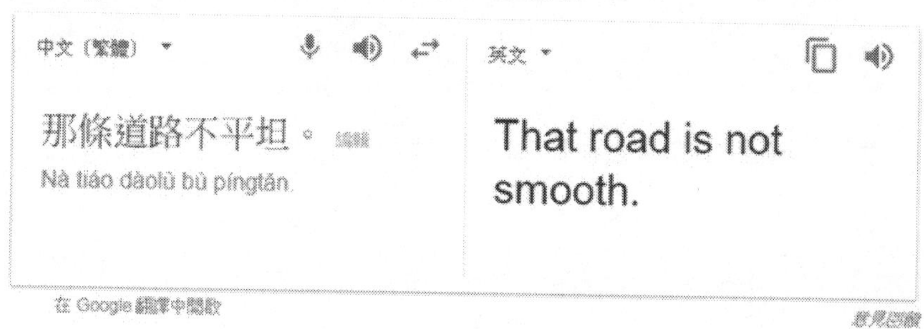

Google 翻譯
https://translate.google.com.tw/?hl=zh-TW
Google 的免費翻譯服務，提供中文和另外上百種語言的互譯功能，讓你即時翻譯字句和網頁內容。

(Image make by author.)

Copy the sentence.

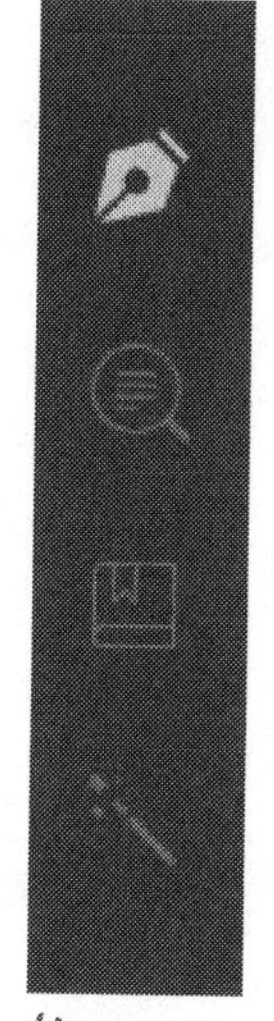

Mary likes to play the piano.

I usually go shopping wearing a hat.

Sir, do you want coffee or drinks?

When I go out in winter, I wear the boots.

That road is not smooth.

(Image make by author.)

Paste the sentence.

The grammar that represents the sentence is correct when no prompt appears.

(Image make by author.)

Copy the sentence.

When I go out in winter, I wear the boots.

That road is not smooth.

I passed the street, often slipped.

(Image make by author.)

Paste the sentence.

The grammar that represents the sentence is correct when no prompt appears.

中文 (繁體)

英文

剛剛小偷經過偷走了那位女士口袋裡的錢包。

Gānggāng xiǎotōu jīngguò tōu zǒule nà wèi nǚshì kǒudài lǐ de qiánbāo.

Just thief stole the purse from the woman's pocket.

在 Google 翻譯中開啟

意見回饋

Google 翻譯

https://translate.google.com.tw/?hl=zh-TW

Google 的免費翻譯服務，提供中文和另外上百種語言的互譯功能，讓你即時翻譯字句和網頁內容。

(Image make by author.)

Copy the sentence.

Sir, do you want coffee or drinks?

When I go out in winter, I wear the boots.

That road is not smooth.

I passed the street, often slipped.

Just thief stole the purse from the woman's pocket.

(Image make by author.)

Paste the sentence.

The grammar that represents the sentence is correct when no prompt appears.

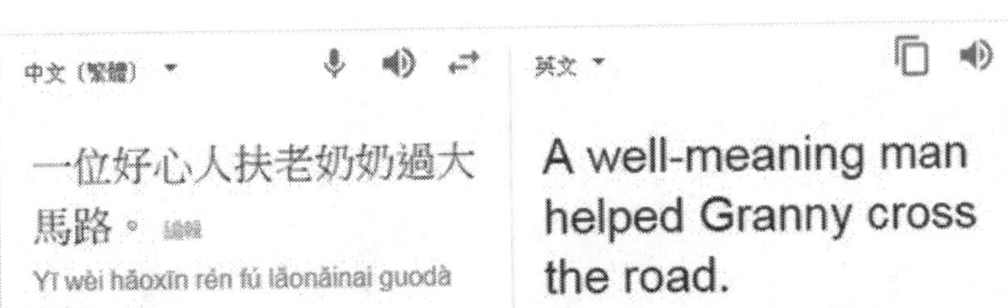

在 Google 翻譯中開啟 意見回饋

Google 翻譯
https://translate.google.com.tw/?hl=zh-TW
Google 的免費翻譯服務，提供中文和另外上百種語言的互譯功能，讓你即時翻譯字句和網頁內容。

(Image make by author.)

Copy the sentence.

When I go out in winter, I wear the boots.
That road is not smooth.
I passed the street, often slipped.
Just thief stole the purse from the woman's pocket.
A well-meaning man helped Granny cross the road.

(Image make by author.)

Paste the sentence.

The grammar that represents the sentence is correct when no prompt appears.

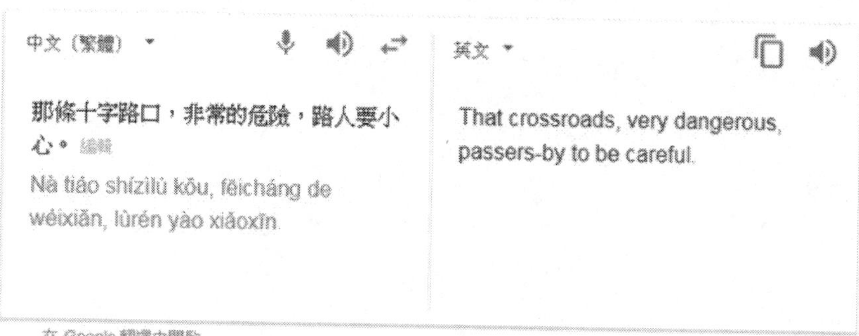

在 Google 翻譯中開啟

意見回饋

Google 翻譯
https://translate.google.com.tw/?hl=zh-TW ▾
Google 的免費翻譯服務，提供中文和另外上百種語言的互譯功能，讓你即時翻譯字句和網頁內容。

(Image make by author.)

Copy the sentence.

Just thief stole the purse from the woman's pocket.
A well-meaning man helped Granny cross the road.
That crossroads, very dangerous, passers-by to be careful.

(Image make by author.)

Paste the sentence.

The grammar that represents the sentence is correct when no prompt appears.

中文（繁體）

英文

我來到港口買了兩張搭船的票。

Wǒ lái dào gǎngkǒu mǎile liǎng zhāng dā chuán de piào.

I came to the harbor and bought two tickets for a boat trip.

在 Google 翻譯中開啟 意見回饋

Google 翻譯
https://translate.google.com.tw/?hl=zh-TW
Google 的免費翻譯服務，提供中文和另外上百種語言的互譯功能，讓你即時翻譯字句和網頁內容。

(Image make by author.)

Copy the sentence.

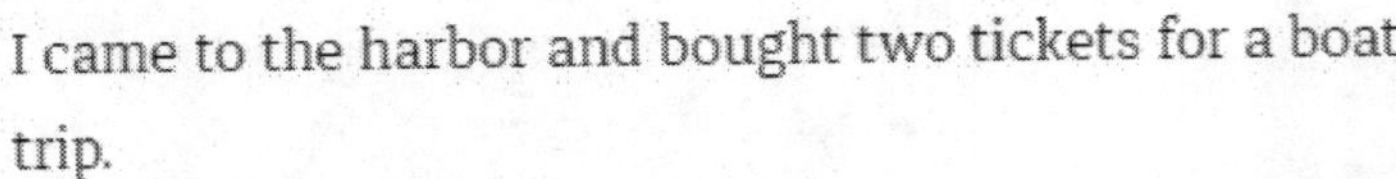

(Image make by author.)

Paste the sentence.

The grammar that represents the sentence is correct when no prompt appears.

中文（繁體）

英文

朋友遲了十分鐘還沒來到。

Péngyǒu chíle shí fēnzhōng hái méi lái dào.

Ten minutes late friend has not arrived yet.

在 Google 翻譯中開啟

意見回饋

Google 翻譯

https://translate.google.com.tw/?hl=zh-TW

Google 的免費翻譯服務，提供中文和另外上百種語言的互譯功能，讓你即時翻譯字句和網頁內容。

(Image make by author.)

Copy the sentence.

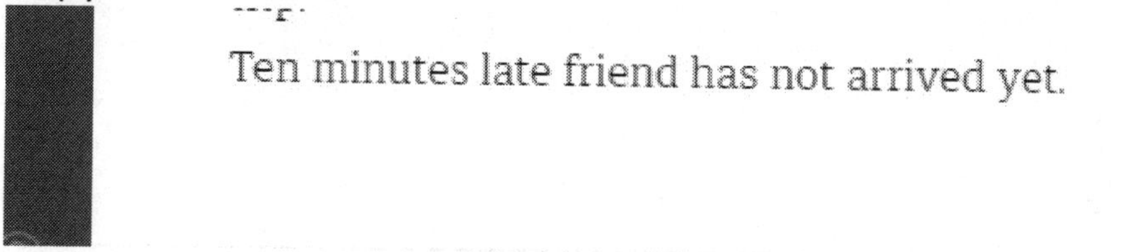

Ten minutes late friend has not arrived yet.

(Image make by author.)

Paste the sentence.

The grammar that represents the sentence is correct when no prompt appears.

中文 (繁體)

英文

我們準備搭船到對岸的小城鎮。

Wǒmen zhǔnbèi dā chuán dào duì'àn de xiǎo chéngzhèn.

We are ready to take a boat to the opposite town.

在 Google 翻譯中開啟

意見回饋

Google 翻譯

https://translate.google.com.tw/?hl=zh-TW

Google 的免費翻譯服務，提供中文和另外上百種語言的互譯功能，讓你即時翻譯字句和網頁內容。

(Image make by author.)

Copy the sentence.

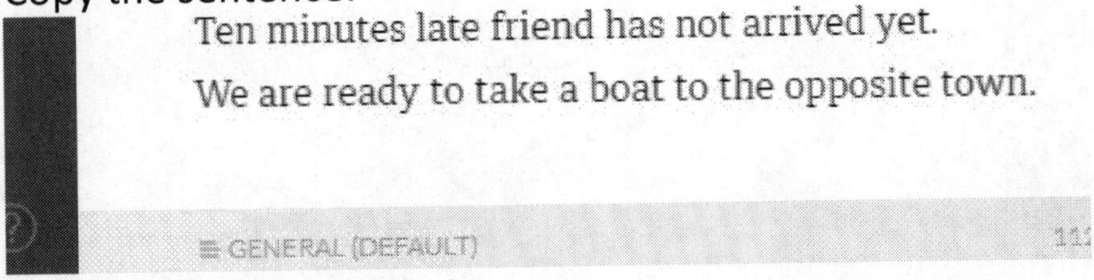

Ten minutes late friend has not arrived yet.

We are ready to take a boat to the opposite town.

≡ GENERAL (DEFAULT)

(Image make by author.)

Paste the sentence.

The grammar that represents the sentence is correct when no prompt appears.

中文（繁體）

英文

那小鎮的風景很好，外國觀光客也常去。 編輯

Nà xiǎo zhèn de fēngjǐng hěn hǎo, wàiguó guānguāng kè yě cháng qù.

The scenery of the town is good, foreign tourists often go.

在 Google 翻譯中開啟

意見回饋

Google 翻譯

https://translate.google.com.tw/?hl=zh-TW

Google 的免費翻譯服務，提供中文和另外上百種語言的互譯功能，讓你即時翻譯字句和網頁內容。

(Image make by author.)

Copy the sentence.

The scenery of the town is good, foreign tourists often go.

GENERAL (DEFAULT)

123 WORDS

(Image make by author.)

Paste the sentence.

The grammar that represents the sentence is correct when no prompt appears.

中文（繁體）

英文

有很多好吃的美食店家，價格都很便宜。 編輯

Yǒu hěnduō hào chī dì měishí diànjiā, jiàgé dōu hěn piányí.

There are many delicious food stores, the prices are very cheap.

在 Google 翻譯中開啟

意見回饋

Google 翻譯

https://translate.google.com.tw/?hl=zh-TW

Google 的免費翻譯服務，提供中文和另外上百種語言的互譯功能，讓你即時翻譯字句和網頁內容。

(Image make by author.)

Copy the sentence.

There are many delicious food stores, the prices are very cheap.

≡ GENERAL (DEFAULT) 134 W

(Image make by author.)

Paste the sentence.

The grammar that represents the sentence is correct when no prompt appears.

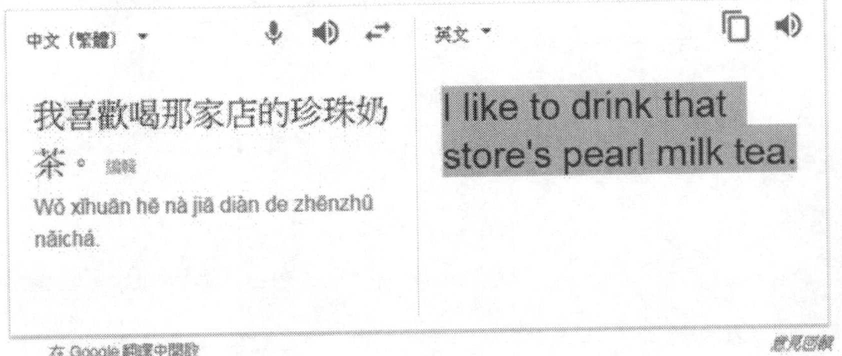

Google 翻譯
https://translate.google.com.tw/?hl=zh-TW
Google 的免費翻譯服務，提供中文和另外上百種語言的互譯功能，讓你即時翻譯字句和網頁內容。

(Image make by author.)

Copy the sentence.

I like to drink that store's pearl milk tea.

≡ GENERAL (DEFAULT)

(Image make by author.)

Paste the sentence.

The grammar that represents the sentence is correct when no prompt appears.

中文 (繁體) ▾ 英文 ▾

那家店的牛肉麵真的是便宜又好吃。 編輯

Nà jiā diàn de niúròu miàn zhēn de shì piányí yòu hào chī.

The beef noodle shop is really cheap and tasty.

在 Google 翻譯中開啟

意見回饋

Google 翻譯

https://translate.google.com.tw/?hl=zh-TW ▾

Google 的免費翻譯服務，提供中文和另外上百種語言的互譯功能，讓你即時翻譯字句和網頁內容。

(Image make by author.)

Copy the sentence.

The beef noodle shop is really cheap and tasty.

≡ GENERAL (DEFAULT)

(Image make by author.)

Paste the sentence.

The grammar that represents the sentence is correct when no prompt appears.

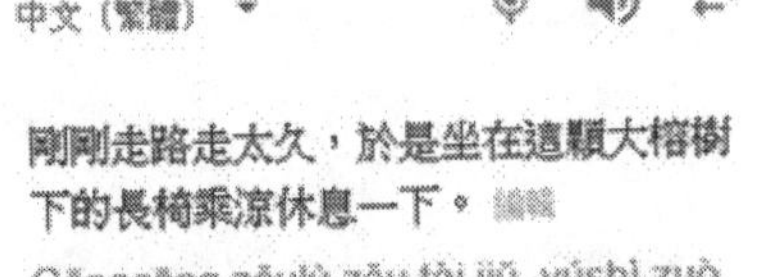

(Image make by author.)

Copy the sentence.

The beef noodle shop is really cheap and tasty.

GENERAL (DEFAULT)

(Image make by author.)

Paste the sentence.

The grammar that represents the sentence is correct when no prompt appears.

After just testing, I found that the quality of translation is mostly grammatically correct.

But occasionally wrong, or do not understand grammar, you can use "Grammarly Tool" as a reference.

-End-

Made in the USA
Columbia, SC
25 May 2022